Poetry of Thought N' *Art*

W. Julian

Copyright © 2012 W. Julian

All rights reserved.

ISBN: 0615438008
ISBN-13: 978-0615438009

This book is dedicated to my Mom,
Sophia Gancarz.
Though she died in 1978 when I was 21.
She adopted me at 4 and
raised me to have faith, love, honor, and
compassion for all things of this planet.
It was her strength, faith, and unconditional love
that gave me life, faith, and hope.
It made me the person I am today.

CONTENTS

	Acknowledgments	I
	Poems	
1	Untitled	1
2	Passion	3
3	Phantom	5
4	Ode to Oprah	9
5	Clone	11
6	Eyes Soul	13
7	Glimpse	17
8	Imprisoned	19
9	Fallen	21
10	Quiet Play	25
11	Freedom's Passion	27
12	Released	29
13	Interlude	33
14	Elements	35
15	Steele	37
16	Threaded	41
17	Life's Meaning	43
18	Flood Gates of Hell	45
19	Ancient and Yet Timeless	49

Photo Art

1	The Mist	7
2	Shadows	15
3	Rebirth	23
4	Timeless	31
5	Root Trees	39
6	Spiritual	47

ACKNOWLEDGMENTS

I would like to thank my family and friends.
I would like to give a special thanks to Patricia
and Bruno, my extended family, you have always
been there and I love you all.
Also I give thanks to my Dear best friends Roseanne,
David, and Michael.
And to my Chatham community, MFA class, new friends
Michael Naismith, Brian Muradi, and all those
who supported me for the last 3 years, while I finished this
book. Thank you for your interest, care, encouragements
and most of all, for pushing me to complete it.
Also a special thanks to Michelle Solomon, my Editor,
Kaitlynn Amber Smith, my Advisor, and
Christina Mongelli, my book Designer.

Dangerous is Desire,
On the Silky wings
Of a dove.
Empty eyes of sorrow,
Dream Excitement.
Thoughts entwine,
Secrets to the Wind.
Where Shines Paradise?

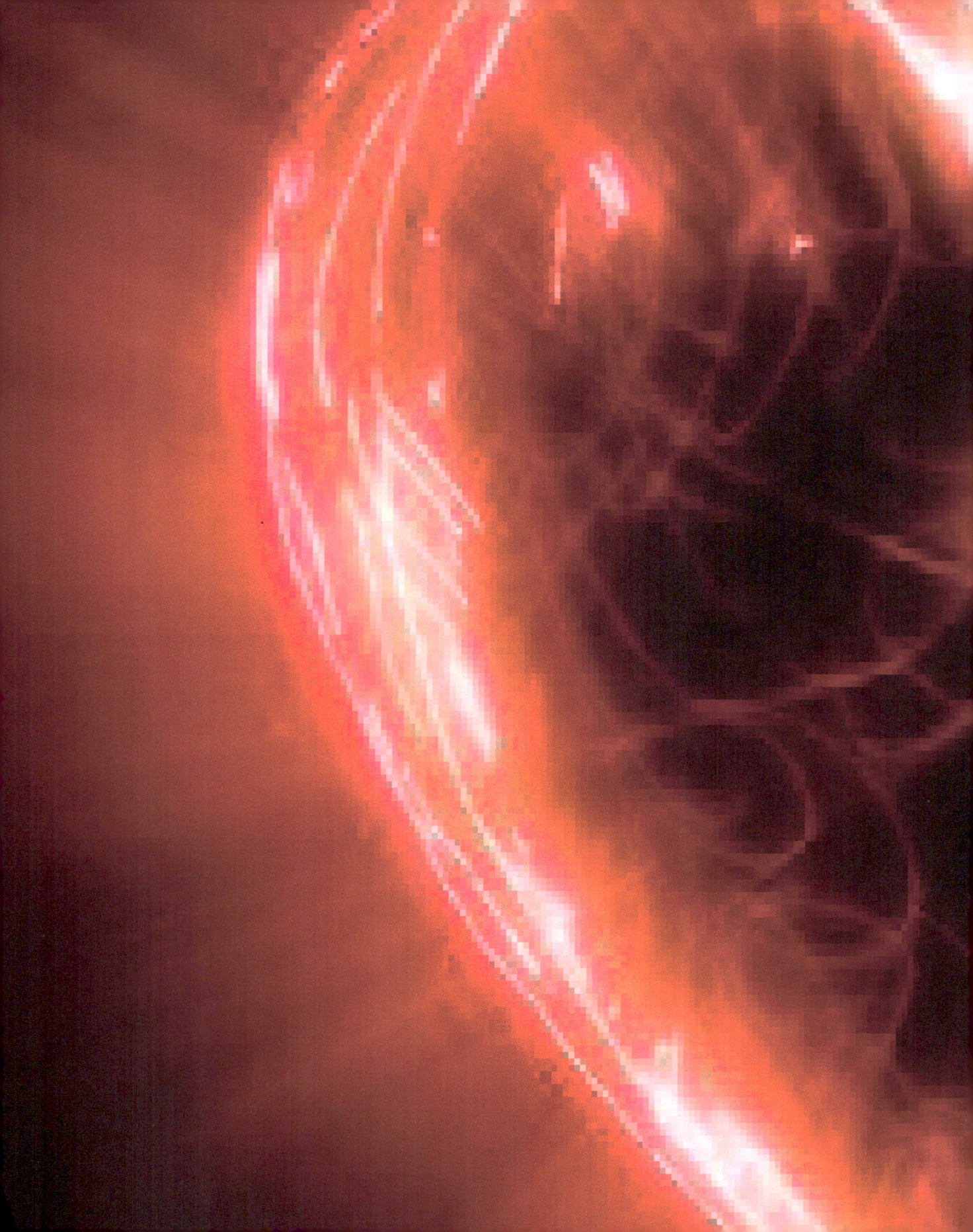

Passion

I have a passion that
Burns deep inside of
Me, for you.
A passion so strong,
That it scares me
A bit.
A passion that I want to
Show and share with you.
A passion, that will always
Be and always grow.
A passion that will wait
For you, to share between us.
A passion that will keep the
Door to my heart, open
To you.
A passion, which can bring us
A lifetime of happiness.
A passion of unconditional Love.

A modern day phantom,
Stands alone.
Stares empty upon the shadows.
Of an unseen copper
Plated hound.
Found entranced upon
The moonlight.

Ode to Oprah

Within her is a Brilliant light.
A light that glows through
every fiber of her being.
It shines brighter than the
brightest star.
Unmatched is her outer
beauty.
Only challenged by the
inner beauty of her soul.
Her wisdom seems timeless.
Her love deeper than the Ocean.
Her understanding is infinite.
She is an open book of honesty
and compassion.
She is all giving and caring.
She is a being of Power, Peace,
Hope and Love.
For all are equal in her eyes.
She is the modern day Mother
Teresa, of our time.
For she is, Oprah!

Clone

Clone Picasso, Degas,
Leonardo and Rembrandt.
Echoes in transitions,
Of modern day wars.
Spells feverishly, of
Outrageous desires.

Eyes Soul

In your eyes, I see love, hope and warmth.
In your eyes, I see understanding and caring.
In your eyes, I see the past, the present
and the future.
In your eyes, I see your dreams and
your goals.
In your eyes, I see your soul.
And In your eyes, I see a frightened
and insecure little boy.
So with your eyes, see through mine.
See the love and understanding I have
for you.
For your past, your present, and
your future.

Glimpse upon the face of a friend.
In whom you have also found a foe.
Behold the sight of a post card.
Then see the truth within your desire.
Look upon the silky web of a spider.
But, ask not what makes it strong.
Soar into the heavens.
Dive into the oceans.
Then walk upon the land.
See the changes in the tide.
The running of both the sun and
the moon.
Look up to the stars.
But, question not ones purpose.
For like that of a circle.
We are all, joined as one.

Imprisoned in a
clown.
Is desire masked by rage.
Screams self-contained
In laughter.
With socially censured
Circumstances.

Fallen are the Seasons.
With forests dying,
Oceans parched.
Gases swaying grasses, hot.
Thoughts today, of yesterday entwined.
Imagined, a more humble life.
Re-arranged spaces and locked doors.
Yet some still filled with pot.
With the poles melting,
Winds rhythmic, splintered.
Northern lights strike, beyond
Time and space.
Across the heavens, awaken the suns fire.
To put us all, in our place.

Quiet play the bells.
Gargoyles roam the
Free world.
Five O'clock desire,
Sometimes hot as hell.
Life found feeling chortle.

Freedom's Passion

On the wings of an Eagle,
We soar into the Heavens.
Then back again.
In this land where freedom was born.
Our souls burn with a passion, deep down inside.
Our hearts desire, what now is hard to find.
With emptiness, we know not how to fill.
As we go on year after year in despair.
As our freedoms are taken by those that claim,
Only theirs is the truth.
We search near and far.
We search for what we cannot find.
Freedom for all!

Released

My body tortured by desire.
Misplaced love pleasured, then broken.
My heart turns from fire to ice.
My senses go numb.
Every fiber of my body breaks down.
And then like that of a soft breeze.
I hear his unmistakable voice.
Then feel a warmth come over my whole body.
Calm settles over all my senses.
My body that once was tortured, by desire.
My love now replaced and unbroken.
My soul now released from within.
Filled with an ever-lasting calm.
A light, that shines so bright.
It cuts through the darkest night.
I am released, released from the tortures
Of desire.

Interlude whispers thoughts,
Of burning desire.
Souls indulging in pleas
Of love.
Soft indigo shadows,
Diffusing logic.
Cries heard passionately
In desperation.

Fire burning,
Storms raging,
Waters churning,
Wind that's racing.
Mother Nature scorned by her children.
God watching intently.
These children's burning desire for
Destruction upon greed.
When will it end?
When will we learn?
We are here to care.
Together to bear,
This burden of a planet so rare.
How much destruction?
How much pain?
How much will we learn?
Before we learn from
The grave.

As you glimpse upon it.
It turns from ice blue to
midnight black.
Sometimes it rises to the sky.
Sometimes it lies flat.
Comes in many a graceful form.
With an almost silky appearance.
It mystifies us near and far.
We take a second glance.
It's sleek; it's hard, but
yet beautiful.
It's mystifying.
It is Steele!

Threaded

Where does one begin?
Where does one end?
Like a needle and thread.
Everything in nature is threaded together.
All things complete the circle.
But when one species decides to mess with
this that circle of life.
Unthread that which is threaded together.
Only God and mother nature decides
that species Fate.
So what will end the human race?
Through greed and by their own hand
So shall end the fate of man.
But the circle of life will start anew.
To bring about a balance that grew.
So then the question stands.
When does one begin?
When does one end?

Life's Meaning

Life is an expression most words could not comprehend
Aiming for acceptance and love of one's self.
Taking it into every aspect of life.
From the smallest morsel of a being
To the largest, casting a shadow over all.
Soaring into the heavens, on silken wings.
A burning passion and desire, deep in one's soul.
It's finding the Holy Grail, within ones heart, through
The power of love and trust.

Filling that void of despair and emptiness.
With hope and kindness towards all.
Living life to its fullest with an endless
Sense of laughter and compassion.
Accepting of an ideal that no one is perfect, except God.
In understanding that true value comes from
The giving of gestures to those in need.
It's making and leaving your mark upon this
world, for a better one.

Flood Gates of Hell

As the flood gates of hell broke.
The demons inside of him arose and awoke.
They took over and controlled his mind.
And mutilated all the decency they could find.
They took control of his life and his limbs.
And they used them for their every whim.
They took him to the counter, to grab a knife.
So they could take another's life.
They took him into the dark shadows of night.
To begin their devilish plight.
And as he looked into the eyes of the victim, they took.
He saw the horror that one only reads in a book.
As he fell to the ground, in despair.
It is his soul that must be repaired.

Ancient and Yet Timeless

He is ancient and yet timeless.
He is nowhere, but yet everywhere.
His wisdom is infinite.
His love is the purest.
His father is the greatest to ever walk the earth.
And as the sun, so too does His light shine ever brighter.
For with just a touch, He can heal.
He has made a few into a multitude.
They are two, yet they are one.
He is God the Father.
He is Jesus Christ the Son.
And in them, all things are possible.

ABOUT THE AUTHOR

   The author was born in 1957 as Wayne Eugene Julian Sullivan but was soon to be adopted 4 years later and lovingly given the name of Wayne Julian Gancarz. Hopewell Pennsylvania became his home for the next 18 years. A love of the arts surfaced early and followed him through life. Always drawing, writing, and taking part in school plays, community theatre, dance or chasing down parts in movies, added excitement and interest to his life.
   Successful in the day to day business world for the next twenty years, the author found himself always searching to find time to add an artist stroke to his nature inspired work or escaping into the world of his love of writing poetry. Even he could see the tie between the beauty of nature in his pictures and the heartfelt words that flowed into a poem. Traveling North, South, East and West, he was always eager to uncover a world of new ideas ready to give birth
   He invites you to take time to find a comfy corner or the open air and ENJOY!

Web: www.wjulians.com

Image Credited

"Blazing Heart." Photo. *google.com* 7 April 2012

   < http://www.google.com>.

"Clone." Photo. *google.com* 7 April 2012

   < http://www.google.com>.

"Passion Art." Photo. *Fantom-xp.com* 7 April 2012

   <http://www.google.com/imgres?q=passion&um=1&hl=en&sa=N&biw=1280&bih=709&tbm=isch&tbnid=_21DdxKLPeeSdM:&imgrefurl=http://www.fantom-xp.com/wp_23__Passion_art_computer_background.html&docid=-XR4eM-rldDadM&imgurl=http://www.fantom-xp.com/wallpapers/23/Passion_art_computer_background.jpg&w=1920&h=1080&ei=DLuET47OBK-I0QHXtr2-Bw&zoom=1&iact=hc&vpx=401&vpy=349&dur=5291&hovh=168&hovw=300&tx=171&ty=191&sig=116780707731734230117&page=2&tbnh=114&tbnw=202&start=19&ndsp=24&ved=1t:429,r:20,s:19,i:237>.

Jørgensen, Bjørn. "Eagle Aurora." Photo. *apod.nasa.gov* 24 Jan. 2012. 7 April 2012

   < http://apod.nasa.gov/apod/ap120124.html>.

Bos, Kaya. Ochoa, Sofia. "Lightning." Photo. *Edublogs.org* 11 April 2011. 7 April 2012

   < http://severeweatherproject.edublogs.org/>.

Silver, David. "By the Sea." Photo. *dwsilver.com* 30 Oct. 2010. 7 April 2012

< http://dwsilver.com/Murphy/2011/By_the_Sea/Wallpaper/>.

www.ingramcontent.com/pod-product-compliance
Lightning Source LLC
Chambersburg PA
CBHW042030150426
43199CB00002B/19